A LIFETIME JOURNAL OF:

I0340003

The Wisdom of Nations:

—

"Wealth may protect a nation, but wisdom preserves a nation."

A GIFT FROM:

Copyright © 2019 by Lizbeth Sharon.

All rights reserved. No part of this publication may be used or reproduced, stored in a retrieval system or transmitted in any form or by any means, electronic, mechanical, photocopying, recording, scanning, or otherwise, except as permitted under Section 107 or 108 of the 1976 United States Copyright Act, without written permission.

The Wisdom of Nations
Lizbeth Sharon

ISBN: 978-0-578-51018-7

Printed in the USA, UK, and Australia

BUT WISDOM PRESERVES A NATION"

Wisdom is as easy as 1-2-3:

#1. Fear God, not people

#2. Hate evil, not people

#3. Repeat

JANUARY 1 ✶ THE WISDOM OF NATIONS

"WEALTH MAY PROTECT A NATION

Godliness makes a nation great.

THE WISDOM OF NATIONS * JANUARY 2

BUT WISDOM PRESERVES A NATION"

Wisdom will make you understand what is right, what is just, and what is fair.

JANUARY 3 * THE WISDOM OF NATIONS

"WEALTH MAY PROTECT A NATION

Wisdom gives a nation length of existence in its right hand and in its left hand wealth and honor.

BUT WISDOM PRESERVES A NATION"

By wisdom the Founding Fathers established the nation. By understanding they set the boundaries in place.

JANUARY 5 �֍ THE WISDOM OF NATIONS

"WEALTH MAY PROTECT A NATION

Wisdom is the foundation of a nation. The better the foundation the higher the nation will rise.

THE WISDOM OF NATIONS � JANUARY 6

BUT WISDOM PRESERVES A NATION"

Only a fool rejects wisdom and good advice. Those who hate wisdom, love death.

JANUARY 7 ✳ THE WISDOM OF NATIONS

"WEALTH MAY PROTECT A NATION

Civilization or the ruin of a nation begins in the homes of its people.

THE WISDOM OF NATIONS * JANUARY 8

BUT WISDOM PRESERVES A NATION"

The world's most violent criminals proved to share one thing: each of them was raised in an argumentative family.

JANUARY 9 * THE WISDOM OF NATIONS

"WEALTH MAY PROTECT A NATION

Govern a family as you would cook a small fish: very gently.

THE WISDOM OF NATIONS * JANUARY 10

Praise the young and they will blossom. Curse the young and they will wither.

"WEALTH MAY PROTECT A NATION

Every morning in Africa, a gazelle wakes up. It knows it must run faster than the fastest lion, or it will be killed. Every morning a lion wakes up. It knows it must run faster than the slowest gazelle, or it will starve to death. It doesn't matter whether you are a lion or a gazelle, when the sun comes up, you better start running.

THE WISDOM OF NATIONS * JANUARY 12

BUT WISDOM PRESERVES A NATION"

Speak the truth always, even it leads to your death.

JANUARY 13 ✷ THE WISDOM OF NATIONS

"WEALTH MAY PROTECT A NATION

The king's justice is better than the country's wealth.

THE WISDOM OF NATIONS ✻ JANUARY 14

BUT WISDOM PRESERVES A NATION"

The wise conceal knowledge, the fools tweet folly.

JANUARY 15 * THE WISDOM OF NATIONS

"WEALTH MAY PROTECT A NATION

Those who get lost on the way to school will never find their way through life.

THE WISDOM OF NATIONS ✷ JANUARY 18

BUT WISDOM PRESERVES A NATION"

When you open a door, don't forget to close it. Treat your mouth accordingly.

JANUARY 19 * THE WISDOM OF NATIONS

"WEALTH MAY PROTECT A NATION

The first
to apologize is
the bravest.
The first
to forgive is
the strongest.
And the first
to forget is
the happiest.

THE WISDOM OF NATIONS ✻ JANUARY 20

BUT WISDOM PRESERVES A NATION"

Get up and don't waste your life. You will be sleeping enough in the grave.

JANUARY 21 * THE WISDOM OF NATIONS

"WEALTH MAY PROTECT A NATION

Feedback,
not criticism.
It takes sweat
to work on things,
but only saliva
to criticize things.

THE WISDOM OF NATIONS ✻ JANUARY 22

BUT WISDOM PRESERVES A NATION"

Use soft words and hard arguments.

JANUARY 23 ✽ THE WISDOM OF NATIONS

"WEALTH MAY PROTECT A NATION

An army of sheep led by a lion would defeat an army of lions led by a sheep.

THE WISDOM OF NATIONS ∗ JANUARY 24

BUT WISDOM PRESERVES A NATION"

Man dies of cold, not of darkness.

JANUARY 25 * THE WISDOM OF NATIONS

"WEALTH MAY PROTECT A NATION

Be careful of your enemy 1X and of your friend 1000X, for a double crossing friend knows more evil.

THE WISDOM OF NATIONS ✴ JANUARY 26

BUT WISDOM PRESERVES A NATION"

Never repay evil for evil. An eye for an eye will make the world go blind.

JANUARY 27 ⁕ THE WISDOM OF NATIONS

"WEALTH MAY PROTECT A NATION

From a wise mind comes wise speech.

THE WISDOM OF NATIONS ✷ JANUARY 28

BUT WISDOM PRESERVES A NATION"

Set
the truth
free,
it will
return
the favor.

JANUARY 29 * THE WISDOM OF NATIONS

"WEALTH MAY PROTECT A NATION

No matter how hot your anger is, it cannot bake bread.

THE WISDOM OF NATIONS * JANUARY 30

BUT WISDOM PRESERVES A NATION"

The wise turns great troubles into little ones, and little ones into none at all.

JANUARY 31 ✷ THE WISDOM OF NATIONS

Good mouth
enjoys
good food,
bad mouth
swallows
bad food.

"WEALTH MAY PROTECT A NATION

Fortune favours the brave, cowards have no luck.

THE WISDOM OF NATIONS ✻ FEBRUARY 2

BUT WISDOM PRESERVES A NATION"

A patient man will eat ripe fruit.

FEBRUARY 3 ❋ THE WISDOM OF NATIONS

"WEALTH MAY PROTECT A NATION

Success and rest do not sleep together.

THE WISDOM OF NATIONS * FEBRUARY 4

BUT WISDOM PRESERVES A NATION"

Character is always corrupted by prosperity.

FEBRUARY 5 ⁕ THE WISDOM OF NATIONS

"WEALTH MAY PROTECT A NATION

Do good to people and you'll enslave their hearts.

THE WISDOM OF NATIONS ✻ FEBRUARY 6

BUT WISDOM PRESERVES A NATION"

A lie has variations, the truth none. Truth has but one color, a lie has many.

FEBRUARY 7 ❋ THE WISDOM OF NATIONS

"WEALTH MAY PROTECT A NATION

Temper gets you into trouble, pride keeps you there.

THE WISDOM OF NATIONS * FEBRUARY 8

BUT WISDOM PRESERVES A NATION"

A lazy shepherd is the wolf's friend.

FEBRUARY 9 ✽ THE WISDOM OF NATIONS

"WEALTH MAY PROTECT A NATION

Ask the young, they know *everything!*

THE WISDOM OF NATIONS * FEBRUARY 10

BUT WISDOM PRESERVES A NATION"

Dishonest king brings discord.

FEBRUARY 11 ⁕ THE WISDOM OF NATIONS

"WEALTH MAY PROTECT A NATION

It is better to die standing than to live bending.

THE WISDOM OF NATIONS ☼ FEBRUARY 12

BUT WISDOM PRESERVES A NATION"

Fall down 7X stand up 8X.

FEBRUARY 13 ✴ THE WISDOM OF NATIONS

"WEALTH MAY PROTECT A NATION

He who begins many things finishes but few.

THE WISDOM OF NATIONS ✷ FEBRUARY 14

BUT WISDOM PRESERVES A NATION"

Listen 100X; think 1000X; speak 1X.

FEBRUARY 15 ✴ THE WISDOM OF NATIONS

"WEALTH MAY PROTECT A NATION

If
I had
8 hours
to chop down
a tree,
I'd spend
6 hours
sharpening
my axe.

THE WISDOM OF NATIONS * FEBRUARY 16

BUT WISDOM PRESERVES A NATION"

You can discover more about a person in an hour of play than in a year of conversation.

FEBRUARY 17 ✶ THE WISDOM OF NATIONS

"WEALTH MAY PROTECT A NATION

Love enters a man through his eyes, woman through her ears.

THE WISDOM OF NATIONS ＊ FEBRUARY 18

BUT WISDOM PRESERVES A NATION"

People show their character by what they laugh at.

FEBRUARY 19 ✶ THE WISDOM OF NATIONS

"WEALTH MAY PROTECT A NATION

Better
1 day
as a lion
than 100
as a sheep.

THE WISDOM OF NATIONS ✻ FEBRUARY 20

BUT WISDOM PRESERVES A NATION"

Rich people never know who their friends are.

FEBRUARY 21 ✷ THE WISDOM OF NATIONS

"WEALTH MAY PROTECT A NATION

Do not look where the harvest is plentiful, but where the people are kind.

THE WISDOM OF NATIONS * FEBRUARY 22

BUT WISDOM PRESERVES A NATION"

A wise man fills his head before emptying his mouth.

FEBRUARY 23 ✵ THE WISDOM OF NATIONS

"WEALTH MAY PROTECT A NATION

Where there is love there is no darkness.

THE WISDOM OF NATIONS �֍ FEBRUARY 24

BUT WISDOM PRESERVES A NATION"

Those who want rain must also accept the mud.

FEBRUARY 25 ✶ THE WISDOM OF NATIONS

"WEALTH MAY PROTECT A NATION

A courageous foe is better than a cowardly friend. Wise enemy is better than a foolish friend.

THE WISDOM OF NATIONS ✻ FEBRUARY 26

BUT WISDOM PRESERVES A NATION"

Vision without action is a daydream. Action without vision is a nightmare.

FEBRUARY 27 ✷ THE WISDOM OF NATIONS

"WEALTH MAY PROTECT A NATION

Anger is the only thing to put off until tomorrow.

THE WISDOM OF NATIONS ✷ FEBRUARY 28

BUT WISDOM PRESERVES A NATION"

A
king
with no
wisdom will
oppress
his people.

FEBRUARY 29 ✷ THE WISDOM OF NATIONS

BUT WISDOM PRESERVES A NATION"

A child that is given everything will rarely succeed in life.

MARCH 1 * THE WISDOM OF NATIONS

"WEALTH MAY PROTECT A NATION

The good wife at her husband's home, the other one is at her parent's home.

THE WISDOM OF NATIONS ✳ MARCH 2

BUT WISDOM PRESERVES A NATION"

Ask your purse what you should buy.

MARCH 3 * THE WISDOM OF NATIONS

"WEALTH MAY PROTECT A NATION

Stay away from fools; they have nothing to teach you.

THE WISDOM OF NATIONS * MARCH 4

BUT WISDOM PRESERVES A NATION"

Examine what is said, not who speaks.

MARCH 5 ✷ THE WISDOM OF NATIONS

"WEALTH MAY PROTECT A NATION

Do not warn a mocker, or he will hate you. Do warn a wise person, and he will love you.

THE WISDOM OF NATIONS * MARCH 6

BUT WISDOM PRESERVES A NATION"

A patient person is better than a warrior. One who controls his temper is better than one who captures a city.

MARCH 7 ✷ THE WISDOM OF NATIONS

"WEALTH MAY PROTECT A NATION

Dead people don't know they're dead, so don't fools.

THE WISDOM OF NATIONS ✲ MARCH 8

BUT WISDOM PRESERVES A NATION"

No time for health today, no health for your time tomorrow.

MARCH 9 ✶ THE WISDOM OF NATIONS

"WEALTH MAY PROTECT A NATION

A great talker is a great liar. Those who know how to praise also know how to lie.

THE WISDOM OF NATIONS * MARCH 10

BUT WISDOM PRESERVES A NATION"

He who refuses to obey cannot command.

MARCH 11 ✱ THE WISDOM OF NATIONS

"WEALTH MAY PROTECT A NATION

Never brag about yourself, let strangers praise you.

THE WISDOM OF NATIONS ✴ **MARCH 12**

BUT WISDOM PRESERVES A NATION"

There's no insurance against death and poverty.

MARCH 13 � THE WISDOM OF NATIONS

"WEALTH MAY PROTECT A NATION

God's help is nearer than the door.

THE WISDOM OF NATIONS ✱ MARCH 14

BUT WISDOM PRESERVES A NATION"

Wisdom is in the head, not in the beard. Intelligence is in the head, not in the age.

MARCH 15 ✷ THE WISDOM OF NATIONS

"WEALTH MAY PROTECT A NATION

Who gossips with you will gossip of you. Listen to what they say of the others and you'll know what they say about you.

THE WISDOM OF NATIONS ✴ MARCH 16

BUT WISDOM PRESERVES A NATION"

Confidence is silent. Insecurities are loud.

MARCH 17 * THE WISDOM OF NATIONS

"WEALTH MAY PROTECT A NATION

A man may live after losing his life but not after losing his honor.

THE WISDOM OF NATIONS ⁕ MARCH 18

BUT WISDOM PRESERVES A NATION"

If your friend becomes your enemy, he will be your enemy for life.

MARCH 19 ✶ THE WISDOM OF NATIONS

"WEALTH MAY PROTECT A NATION

If you think education is expensive, try ignorance.

THE WISDOM OF NATIONS ❊ MARCH 20

BUT WISDOM PRESERVES A NATION"

A person who does not speak out against the wrong is a mute devil.

MARCH 21 ⁕ THE WISDOM OF NATIONS

"WEALTH MAY PROTECT A NATION

Having
2 ears and
1 tongue,
we should
listen
2X as much
as we speak.

THE WISDOM OF NATIONS ✳ MARCH 22

BUT WISDOM PRESERVES A NATION"

A healthy man is a successful man.

MARCH 23 * THE WISDOM OF NATIONS

> **"WEALTH MAY PROTECT A NATION**

When a thief shakes your hand, count your fingers. When a thief kisses you, count your teeth.

THE WISDOM OF NATIONS ✷ MARCH 24

BUT WISDOM PRESERVES A NATION"

A king's mercy and truth will win people's hearts.

MARCH 25 ✶ THE WISDOM OF NATIONS

"WEALTH MAY PROTECT A NATION

The
sun
shines
brighter
after
the rain.

THE WISDOM OF NATIONS * MARCH 26

BUT WISDOM PRESERVES A NATION"

The depth of a person's life is more important than the length.

MARCH 27 * THE WISDOM OF NATIONS

"WEALTH MAY PROTECT A NATION

Visit each other but don't be neighbors.

THE WISDOM OF NATIONS ✻ MARCH 28

BUT WISDOM PRESERVES A NATION"

If you can't resolve your problems in peace, you can't solve war.

MARCH 29 ✶ THE WISDOM OF NATIONS

"WEALTH MAY PROTECT A NATION

Promises make debt. And debt makes promises. Borrow causes sorrow.

THE WISDOM OF NATIONS * MARCH 30

BUT WISDOM PRESERVES A NATION"

Before you ask a man for clothes, look at the clothes he is wearing.

MARCH 31 ＊ THE WISDOM OF NATIONS

BUT WISDOM PRESERVES A NATION"

Never approach a goat from the front, a horse from the back, or a fool from any side.

APRIL 1 ✲ THE WISDOM OF NATIONS

"WEALTH MAY PROTECT A NATION

Being happy is better than being king.

THE WISDOM OF NATIONS ✶ APRIL 2

BUT WISDOM PRESERVES A NATION"

He who comes with a story to you brings two away from you.

APRIL 3 ✶ THE WISDOM OF NATIONS

"WEALTH MAY PROTECT A NATION

Where the tongue slips, it speaks the truth.

THE WISDOM OF NATIONS ✵ APRIL 4

BUT WISDOM PRESERVES A NATION"

Beware of still water, a still dog, and a still enemy.

APRIL 5 ✷ THE WISDOM OF NATIONS

"WEALTH MAY PROTECT A NATION

Bricks and mortar make a house, but the laughter of children make a home.

THE WISDOM OF NATIONS * APRIL 6

BUT WISDOM PRESERVES A NATION"

A long skirt wraps around the leg, a long tongue wraps around the head.

APRIL 7 ∗ THE WISDOM OF NATIONS

"WEALTH MAY PROTECT A NATION

A handful of patience is worth more than a bushel of brains.

THE WISDOM OF NATIONS * APRIL 8

BUT WISDOM PRESERVES A NATION"

It's
better
to have
less thunder
in the mouth and
more lightning
in the hand.

APRIL 9 * THE WISDOM OF NATIONS

"WEALTH MAY PROTECT A NATION

Cross the loud river, but don't cross the silent one.

THE WISDOM OF NATIONS * APRIL 10

BUT WISDOM PRESERVES A NATION"

One moment of patience may ward off great disaster. One moment of impatience may ruin a whole life.

APRIL 11 ✳ THE WISDOM OF NATIONS

> "WEALTH MAY PROTECT A NATION

People with good intentions make promises, but people with good character keep them.

THE WISDOM OF NATIONS * **APRIL 12**

BUT WISDOM PRESERVES A NATION"

Let's sit bent, but talk straight.

APRIL 13 ✻ THE WISDOM OF NATIONS

"WEALTH MAY PROTECT A NATION

You can't rebound if you don't hit bottom.

THE WISDOM OF NATIONS ✷ APRIL 14

BUT WISDOM PRESERVES A NATION"

1 dishonesty ruins 1000 honesties. You tell 1 dishonesty and all your honesties become questionable.

APRIL 15 ✲ THE WISDOM OF NATIONS

"WEALTH MAY PROTECT A NATION

You learn a lot about a man by his behavior when hungry.

THE WISDOM OF NATIONS ☆ APRIL 16

BUT WISDOM PRESERVES A NATION"

Home is where life is found in its fullness.

APRIL 17 ✷ THE WISDOM OF NATIONS

"WEALTH MAY PROTECT A NATION

A good thing sells itself, a bad one advertises itself.

THE WISDOM OF NATIONS ✻ **APRIL 18**

BUT WISDOM PRESERVES A NATION"

Patience is the most necessary qualification for a business. A man'd rather you heard his story than granted his request.

APRIL 19 * THE WISDOM OF NATIONS

"WEALTH MAY PROTECT A NATION

Choose your neighbors before choosing your home. A good neighbor increases the value of your property.

THE WISDOM OF NATIONS * APRIL 20

BUT WISDOM PRESERVES A NATION"

Your greatness is not what you have, it's what you give.

APRIL 21 ✻ THE WISDOM OF NATIONS

"WEALTH MAY PROTECT A NATION

In the midst of great joy, do not promise anyone anything. In the midst of great anger, do not answer anyone's letter.

THE WISDOM OF NATIONS * APRIL 22

BUT WISDOM PRESERVES A NATION"

You
rise
by
lifting
others.

APRIL 23 ✴ THE WISDOM OF NATIONS

"WEALTH MAY PROTECT A NATION

Share your plans with God and you will succeed!

THE WISDOM OF NATIONS * APRIL 24

BUT WISDOM PRESERVES A NATION"

No one has ever become poor by giving.

APRIL 25 ✻ THE WISDOM OF NATIONS

"WEALTH MAY PROTECT A NATION

If
you want
to go fast,
go alone.
If you want
to go far,
go together.

THE WISDOM OF NATIONS ✻ APRIL 26

BUT WISDOM PRESERVES A NATION"

A pretty face and fine clothes do not make character.

APRIL 27 ✻ THE WISDOM OF NATIONS

"WEALTH MAY PROTECT A NATION

To know the road ahead, ask those coming back.

THE WISDOM OF NATIONS ✶ APRIL 28

BUT WISDOM PRESERVES A NATION"

The greatest joy comes from freely giving.

APRIL 29 ✳ THE WISDOM OF NATIONS

"WEALTH MAY PROTECT A NATION

Do bad and remember, do good and forget.

THE WISDOM OF NATIONS ☆ APRIL 30

BUT WISDOM PRESERVES A NATION"

When kings lose direction, they become servants.

MAY 1 * THE WISDOM OF NATIONS

"WEALTH MAY PROTECT A NATION

There
is
a secure
fortress
in the fear
of God.

THE WISDOM OF NATIONS ✵ MAY 2

BUT WISDOM PRESERVES A NATION"

A dog that barks all the time gets little attention.

MAY 3 ✷ THE WISDOM OF NATIONS

"WEALTH MAY PROTECT A NATION

A plan in the heart of a man is like deep water, only a wise man will draw it out.

THE WISDOM OF NATIONS * MAY 4

BUT WISDOM PRESERVES A NATION"

Everyone is wise 'til he speaks.

MAY 5 ✱ THE WISDOM OF NATIONS

"WEALTH MAY PROTECT A NATION

Only
by giving
are you able
to receive
more than
you already
have.

THE WISDOM OF NATIONS * MAY 6

BUT WISDOM PRESERVES A NATION"

No woman can make a wise man out of a fool, but every woman can change a wise man into a fool.

MAY 7 ✲ THE WISDOM OF NATIONS

"WEALTH MAY PROTECT A NATION

The darkest hour is just before the dawn. In the time of darkest defeat, victory may be nearest.

THE WISDOM OF NATIONS * MAY 8

BUT WISDOM PRESERVES A NATION"

Wealth diminishes with use, but learning increases with use.

MAY 9 * THE WISDOM OF NATIONS

"WEALTH MAY PROTECT A NATION

Before preparing to improve the world, first look around your own home 3X.

THE WISDOM OF NATIONS ✸ MAY 10

BUT WISDOM PRESERVES A NATION"

If you educate a man, you educate an individual. But, if you educate a woman, you educate a nation.

MAY 11 ✷ THE WISDOM OF NATIONS

"WEALTH MAY PROTECT A NATION

Talking comes by nature, silence by wisdom.

THE WISDOM OF NATIONS ✷ MAY 12

BUT WISDOM PRESERVES A NATION"

Complaining is the weak's weapon.

MAY 13 * **THE WISDOM OF NATIONS**

"WEALTH MAY PROTECT A NATION

The only sword that never rests is the tongue of a woman.

THE WISDOM OF NATIONS * MAY 14

BUT WISDOM PRESERVES A NATION"

Life can't be trusted, death can come at any moment.

MAY 15 ✶ THE WISDOM OF NATIONS

"WEALTH MAY PROTECT A NATION

Visit rarely, and you will be more loved. Even the best song becomes tiresome if heard too often.

THE WISDOM OF NATIONS * MAY 16

BUT WISDOM PRESERVES A NATION"

Give freely and become more wealthy; be stingy and lose everything. Sometimes you can become rich by being generous or poor by being greedy.

MAY 17 * THE WISDOM OF NATIONS

"WEALTH MAY PROTECT A NATION

Patience is a plant that does not grow in everyone's garden.

THE WISDOM OF NATIONS * MAY 18

BUT WISDOM PRESERVES A NATION"

When the character of a man is not clear to you, look at his friends.

MAY 19 * THE WISDOM OF NATIONS

"WEALTH MAY PROTECT A NATION

Kind words do not wear out the tongue.

THE WISDOM OF NATIONS ☆ MAY 20

BUT WISDOM PRESERVES A NATION"

In the moments of crisis, the wise build bridges and the foolish build dams.

MAY 21 ✳ THE WISDOM OF NATIONS

"WEALTH MAY PROTECT A NATION

Never strike your wife, even with a flower.

THE WISDOM OF NATIONS ✻ **MAY 22**

BUT WISDOM PRESERVES A NATION"

You could always lock your door from a darn thief, but not from a darn liar.

MAY 23 ＊ THE WISDOM OF NATIONS

"WEALTH MAY PROTECT A NATION

Better give a penny than lend twenty.

THE WISDOM OF NATIONS * MAY 24

BUT WISDOM PRESERVES A NATION"

Proof, not argument.

MAY 25 ❊ THE WISDOM OF NATIONS

"WEALTH MAY PROTECT A NATION

Flies can't fly into a closed mouth.

THE WISDOM OF NATIONS ✱ MAY 26

BUT WISDOM PRESERVES A NATION"

Life is for one generation; a good name is forever.

MAY 27 ✴ THE WISDOM OF NATIONS

"WEALTH MAY PROTECT A NATION

Beauty without virtue is a curse.

THE WISDOM OF NATIONS ✴ MAY 28

BUT WISDOM PRESERVES A NATION"

Dig the well before you are thirsty.

MAY 29 * THE WISDOM OF NATIONS

"WEALTH MAY PROTECT A NATION

Books are preserved minds.

THE WISDOM OF NATIONS * MAY 30

BUT WISDOM PRESERVES A NATION"

An
hour
of adultery,
a lifetime
of disgrace.

MAY 31 ✻ THE WISDOM OF NATIONS

BUT WISDOM PRESERVES A NATION"

Some people are always greedy for more, but the godly love to give! People who obey God are always generous.

JUNE 1 * THE WISDOM OF NATIONS

"WEALTH MAY PROTECT A NATION

Stop looking for a happiness in the same place you lost it.

THE WISDOM OF NATIONS * JUNE 2

BUT WISDOM PRESERVES A NATION"

We rest our legs, but never our mouths.

JUNE 3 ✷ THE WISDOM OF NATIONS

"WEALTH MAY PROTECT A NATION

The way a man eats is the way he works.

THE WISDOM OF NATIONS * JUNE 4

BUT WISDOM PRESERVES A NATION"

You have a lifetime to work, but children are only young once.

JUNE 5 ✳ THE WISDOM OF NATIONS

"WEALTH MAY PROTECT A NATION

There are three things you can't hide: coughing, poverty, and love.

THE WISDOM OF NATIONS * JUNE 6

BUT WISDOM PRESERVES A NATION"

In the struggle between the stone and water; in time, the water wins.

JUNE 7 ✶ THE WISDOM OF NATIONS

"WEALTH MAY PROTECT A NATION

Never trust the advice of a man in difficulties.

THE WISDOM OF NATIONS ✴ JUNE 8

BUT WISDOM PRESERVES A NATION"

Live together like brothers and do business like strangers.

JUNE 9 ✷ THE WISDOM OF NATIONS

> "WEALTH MAY PROTECT A NATION

When you get older you keep warm with the wood you gathered as a youth.

BUT WISDOM PRESERVES A NATION"

The wise person has long ears and a short tongue.

JUNE 11 ✶ THE WISDOM OF NATIONS

"WEALTH MAY PROTECT A NATION

Cold tea and cold rice are tolerable; cold looks and cold words aren't.

THE WISDOM OF NATIONS ✱ JUNE 12

BUT WISDOM PRESERVES A NATION"

He
who
is guilty
has much
to say.

JUNE 13 ✳ THE WISDOM OF NATIONS

"WEALTH MAY PROTECT A NATION

You
are
not born
a leader,
you
become
one.

THE WISDOM OF NATIONS * JUNE 14

BUT WISDOM PRESERVES A NATION"

Many complain of their looks, but none of their brains.

JUNE 15 ※ THE WISDOM OF NATIONS

"WEALTH MAY PROTECT A NATION

1 father is more than 100 teachers.

THE WISDOM OF NATIONS * JUNE 16

BUT WISDOM PRESERVES A NATION"

If someone throws stones at you, throw back bread.

JUNE 17 ٭ THE WISDOM OF NATIONS

"WEALTH MAY PROTECT A NATION

The day
you decide
to do it
is your
lucky day.

THE WISDOM OF NATIONS * JUNE 18

BUT WISDOM PRESERVES A NATION"

You take a bull by its horns and a man by his words.

JUNE 19 * THE WISDOM OF NATIONS

"WEALTH MAY PROTECT A NATION

Make happy those who are near, and those who are far will come.

THE WISDOM OF NATIONS * JUNE 20

BUT WISDOM PRESERVES A NATION"

Blessed are those who are generous, because they feed the poor.

JUNE 21 ✶ THE WISDOM OF NATIONS

"WEALTH MAY PROTECT A NATION

If
you want
your dreams
to come true,
don't oversleep.

THE WISDOM OF NATIONS ⁕ JUNE 22

BUT WISDOM PRESERVES A NATION"

We are no more than candles burning in the wind.

JUNE 23 ✳ THE WISDOM OF NATIONS

"WEALTH MAY PROTECT A NATION

Love your neighbors, but don't pull down the fence. A lock is better than suspicion.

THE WISDOM OF NATIONS * JUNE 24

BUT WISDOM PRESERVES A NATION"

Your secret is your blood, when you shed it you die.

JUNE 25 * THE WISDOM OF NATIONS

"WEALTH MAY PROTECT A NATION

A
brave man
seldom
is hurt
in the back.

THE WISDOM OF NATIONS ✲ JUNE 26

BUT WISDOM PRESERVES A NATION"

What you don't see with your eyes, don't invent with your mouth.

JUNE 27 ✶ THE WISDOM OF NATIONS

"WEALTH MAY PROTECT A NATION

Old people are everyone's treasures.

THE WISDOM OF NATIONS * JUNE 28

BUT WISDOM PRESERVES A NATION"

Even if you encounter a stone bridge, tap it first before crossing.

JUNE 29 ✷ THE WISDOM OF NATIONS

"WEALTH MAY PROTECT A NATION

A
half-truth
is
a whole lie.

THE WISDOM OF NATIONS ✷ JUNE 30

BUT WISDOM PRESERVES A NATION"

If a beautiful woman is a jewel, then a good woman is a treasure.

JULY 1 * THE WISDOM OF NATIONS

"WEALTH MAY PROTECT A NATION

Never trust your friend with a secret. A secret for two is soon a secret for nobody.

THE WISDOM OF NATIONS ✢ JULY 2

BUT WISDOM PRESERVES A NATION"

Don't be too sweet lest you be eaten up; don't be too bitter lest you be spewed out.

JULY 3 ✶ THE WISDOM OF NATIONS

"WEALTH MAY PROTECT A NATION

A nation without God's guidance is a nation without order.

THE WISDOM OF NATIONS ✷ JULY 4

BUT WISDOM PRESERVES A NATION"

Be slow in choosing a friend but slower in changing him.

JULY 5 ✳ THE WISDOM OF NATIONS

"WEALTH MAY PROTECT A NATION

Wounds heal, but not ill words.

THE WISDOM OF NATIONS ٭ JULY 6

BUT WISDOM PRESERVES A NATION"

Better to be slapped with the truth than kissed with a lie.

JULY 7 ✵ THE WISDOM OF NATIONS

"WEALTH MAY PROTECT A NATION

Never promise a poor person, and never owe a rich one.

THE WISDOM OF NATIONS * JULY 8

BUT WISDOM PRESERVES A NATION"

A
little help
is better than
a lot of pity.

JULY 9 ✵ THE WISDOM OF NATIONS

"WEALTH MAY PROTECT A NATION

He who lies for you will also lie against you.

THE WISDOM OF NATIONS * JULY 10

BUT WISDOM PRESERVES A NATION"

A chattering bird builds no nest. A roaring lion does not catch any prey.

JULY 11 * THE WISDOM OF NATIONS

"WEALTH MAY PROTECT A NATION

Do not choose your wife at a dance, but in the field among the harvesters.

THE WISDOM OF NATIONS ✻ JULY 12

BUT WISDOM PRESERVES A NATION"

Giving to the poor will keep you from poverty, but those who close their eyes to poverty will be cursed.

JULY 13 * THE WISDOM OF NATIONS

"WEALTH MAY PROTECT A NATION

Wisdom, common sense, and knowledge are BFF.

THE WISDOM OF NATIONS ✻ JULY 14

BUT WISDOM PRESERVES A NATION"

Keep evil advisers away from the king, and his throne will be established in righteousness.

"WEALTH MAY PROTECT A NATION

Little and often fills the purse.

THE WISDOM OF NATIONS ❋ JULY 16

BUT WISDOM PRESERVES A NATION"

A house with two keys is worth nothing. Two captains sink the ship.

JULY 17 ❊ THE WISDOM OF NATIONS

"WEALTH MAY PROTECT A NATION

The soul would have no rainbow if the eyes had no tears.

THE WISDOM OF NATIONS ✱ JULY 18

BUT WISDOM PRESERVES A NATION"

If and When were planted, then Nothing grew.

JULY 19 ✷ THE WISDOM OF NATIONS

"WEALTH MAY PROTECT A NATION

One cannot both feast and become rich.

THE WISDOM OF NATIONS * JULY 20

BUT WISDOM PRESERVES A NATION"

A lie can take you far away but with no hope of return.

JULY 21 ✲ THE WISDOM OF NATIONS

"WEALTH MAY PROTECT A NATION

No one can please God without faith. Whoever comes to God must believe that God exists and rewards those who seek Him.

THE WISDOM OF NATIONS ✳ **JULY 22**

BUT WISDOM PRESERVES A NATION"

Kindness will never be wasted in any way.

JULY 23 ✶ THE WISDOM OF NATIONS

"WEALTH MAY PROTECT A NATION

No matter how far you have gone on the wrong road, turn back.

THE WISDOM OF NATIONS ✻ JULY 24

BUT WISDOM PRESERVES A NATION"

Too humble is half proud.

JULY 25 * THE WISDOM OF NATIONS

"WEALTH MAY PROTECT A NATION

Never marry for money. Ye'll borrow it cheaper.

THE WISDOM OF NATIONS ✷ JULY 26

BUT WISDOM PRESERVES A NATION"

If you understand everything, you must be misinformed.

JULY 27 ✵ THE WISDOM OF NATIONS

"WEALTH MAY PROTECT A NATION

If you take too long to choose, you will end up with the leftovers.

THE WISDOM OF NATIONS ✵ JULY 28

BUT WISDOM PRESERVES A NATION"

There is no right way to do a wrong thing.

JULY 29 * THE WISDOM OF NATIONS

"WEALTH MAY PROTECT A NATION

When a ripe fruit sees an honest man, it drops.

THE WISDOM OF NATIONS * JULY 30

BUT WISDOM PRESERVES A NATION"

Pride goes only as far as one can spit.

JULY 31 ※ THE WISDOM OF NATIONS

BUT WISDOM PRESERVES A NATION"

If a child is uneducated, the father is to blame.

AUGUST 1 ✱ THE WISDOM OF NATIONS

"WEALTH MAY PROTECT A NATION

The best trees grow on the steepest hills.

THE WISDOM OF NATIONS * AUGUST 2

BUT WISDOM PRESERVES A NATION"

A friend that can be bought is not worth buying.

AUGUST 3 * THE WISDOM OF NATIONS

> "WEALTH MAY PROTECT A NATION

Traveler, there are no paths. Paths are made by walking.

THE WISDOM OF NATIONS * AUGUST 4

BUT WISDOM PRESERVES A NATION"

There is no better mirror than the face of an old friend.

AUGUST 5 ⁕ THE WISDOM OF NATIONS

"WEALTH MAY PROTECT A NATION

After the game, the king and the pawn go into the same box.

THE WISDOM OF NATIONS * AUGUST 6

BUT WISDOM PRESERVES A NATION"

Do what your teacher says but not what he does.

AUGUST 7 ✻ THE WISDOM OF NATIONS

"WEALTH MAY PROTECT A NATION

Sorrow is like a precious treasure, shown only to friends.

THE WISDOM OF NATIONS * AUGUST 8

BUT WISDOM PRESERVES A NATION"

A slave shows his true character, not while he is enslaved but when he becomes a master.

AUGUST 9 * THE WISDOM OF NATIONS

"WEALTH MAY PROTECT A NATION

Patience is waiting. Not passively waiting. That is laziness. But to keep going when the going is hard and slow.

THE WISDOM OF NATIONS ✷ AUGUST 10

BUT WISDOM PRESERVES A NATION"

Do not protect yourself with a fence, but rather by your friends.

AUGUST 11 ✶ THE WISDOM OF NATIONS

"WEALTH MAY PROTECT A NATION

You must
judge
a woman
by the taste
of her soup.

THE WISDOM OF NATIONS ✷ AUGUST 12

BUT WISDOM PRESERVES A NATION"

Don't give your strength to women or your power to those who ruin kings.

AUGUST 13 ✱ THE WISDOM OF NATIONS

"WEALTH MAY PROTECT A NATION

If you refuse to be made straight when you are green, you will not be made straight when you are dry.

THE WISDOM OF NATIONS ∗ AUGUST 14

BUT WISDOM PRESERVES A NATION"

When a man is not a lover in his twenties, not strong in his thirties, not rich in his forties, and not wise in his fifties; he'll never be so.

AUGUST 15 * THE WISDOM OF NATIONS

"WEALTH MAY PROTECT A NATION

If you have 5 wives then you will have 5 tongues.

THE WISDOM OF NATIONS * AUGUST 16

BUT WISDOM PRESERVES A NATION"

A chatterbox
is
a treasure
for a spy.

AUGUST 17 * THE WISDOM OF NATIONS

"WEALTH MAY PROTECT A NATION

When you throw dirt, you lose ground. When you keep your tongue, you keep yourself out of trouble.

THE WISDOM OF NATIONS ✻ AUGUST 18

BUT WISDOM PRESERVES A NATION"

A silent man is the best one to listen to.

AUGUST 19 ✢ THE WISDOM OF NATIONS

"WEALTH MAY PROTECT A NATION

The strong forgive, the weak remember.

THE WISDOM OF NATIONS * AUGUST 20

BUT WISDOM PRESERVES A NATION"

Do not say the first thing that comes to your mind.

AUGUST 21 ✶ THE WISDOM OF NATIONS

"WEALTH MAY PROTECT A NATION

After three days, both fish and guests begin to smell.

THE WISDOM OF NATIONS ✻ AUGUST 22

BUT WISDOM PRESERVES A NATION"

A bamboo that bends is stronger than the oak that resists.

AUGUST 23 ⁕ THE WISDOM OF NATIONS

"WEALTH MAY PROTECT A NATION

Familiarity breeds contempt; distance breeds respect.

THE WISDOM OF NATIONS ✲ AUGUST 24

BUT WISDOM PRESERVES A NATION"

Eggs may be smarter than the chickens, but it doesn't take long for them to stink.

AUGUST 25 ∗ THE WISDOM OF NATIONS

"WEALTH MAY PROTECT A NATION

The primary determinant of success is mindset. Not talent. Not experience.

THE WISDOM OF NATIONS ✲ AUGUST 26

BUT WISDOM PRESERVES A NATION"

Everything you were taught in life can be put into a few words: Respect and obey God! This is what life is all about.

AUGUST 27 * THE WISDOM OF NATIONS

"WEALTH MAY PROTECT A NATION

Bad habits are easier to abandon today than tomorrow.

THE WISDOM OF NATIONS ✷ AUGUST 28

BUT WISDOM PRESERVES A NATION"

If you're a beggar for three days, you won't be able to stop.

AUGUST 29 * THE WISDOM OF NATIONS

"WEALTH MAY PROTECT A NATION

Give advice; if people don't listen, let adversity teach them.

THE WISDOM OF NATIONS ✽ AUGUST 30

BUT WISDOM PRESERVES A NATION"

In giving advice: seek to help, not to please.

AUGUST 31 * THE WISDOM OF NATIONS

BUT WISDOM PRESERVES A NATION"

Unclean words come from unclean heart.

SEPTEMBER 1 ✲ THE WISDOM OF NATIONS

"WEALTH MAY PROTECT A NATION

Distance tests a horse's strength. Time reveals a person's character.

THE WISDOM OF NATIONS ✳ SEPTEMBER 2

BUT WISDOM PRESERVES A NATION"

Divorce is the sacrament of adultery.

SEPTEMBER 3 ✳ THE WISDOM OF NATIONS

"WEALTH MAY PROTECT A NATION

Flies' legs, like the tongue of critics, land on whatever they find.

THE WISDOM OF NATIONS * SEPTEMBER 4

BUT WISDOM PRESERVES A NATION"

The best time to plant a tree is 20 years ago. The second best time is now.

SEPTEMBER 5 ✴ THE WISDOM OF NATIONS

"WEALTH MAY PROTECT A NATION

Time doesn't change. Time reveals.

THE WISDOM OF NATIONS * SEPTEMBER 6

BUT WISDOM PRESERVES A NATION"

Don't throw stones at your neighbors if your own windows are glass.

SEPTEMBER 7 ✶ THE WISDOM OF NATIONS

"WEALTH MAY PROTECT A NATION

A man who uses force is afraid of reasoning.

THE WISDOM OF NATIONS * SEPTEMBER 8

BUT WISDOM PRESERVES A NATION"

If you close your eyes to facts, you will learn through accidents.

SEPTEMBER 9 ✳ THE WISDOM OF NATIONS

"WEALTH MAY PROTECT A NATION

Learning is a treasure that will follow its owner everywhere.

THE WISDOM OF NATIONS * SEPTEMBER 10

BUT WISDOM PRESERVES A NATION"

Purchase truth, but don't sell it; store up wisdom, instruction, and understanding.

SEPTEMBER 11 ✻ THE WISDOM OF NATIONS

"WEALTH MAY PROTECT A NATION

If a child washes his hands he could eat with kings.

THE WISDOM OF NATIONS * SEPTEMBER 12

BUT WISDOM PRESERVES A NATION"

When
we are
at our
happiest,
then it
is best
to leave
and go home.

SEPTEMBER 13 * THE WISDOM OF NATIONS

"WEALTH MAY PROTECT A NATION

Opportunities always look bigger going than coming.

THE WISDOM OF NATIONS ✶ SEPTEMBER 14

BUT WISDOM PRESERVES A NATION"

Don't spend the evening in a house where you can't spend the night.

SEPTEMBER 15 ✶ THE WISDOM OF NATIONS

"WEALTH MAY PROTECT A NATION

A wise man changes his mind, a fool never will.

THE WISDOM OF NATIONS * SEPTEMBER 16

BUT WISDOM PRESERVES A NATION"

Fearing people is a dangerous trap, but trusting God means safety.

SEPTEMBER 17 ✶ THE WISDOM OF NATIONS

"WEALTH MAY PROTECT A NATION

Don't make friends with a hot-tempered person, or you will learn their ways and set a trap for yourself.

THE WISDOM OF NATIONS * SEPTEMBER 18

BUT WISDOM PRESERVES A NATION"

If you marry a monkey for his wealth, the money goes and the monkey remains as is.

SEPTEMBER 19 ✳ THE WISDOM OF NATIONS

"WEALTH MAY PROTECT A NATION

Consider the tune, not the voice; consider the words, not the tune; consider the meaning, not the words.

THE WISDOM OF NATIONS ✶ SEPTEMBER 20

BUT WISDOM PRESERVES A NATION"

Kind words will unlock an iron door.

SEPTEMBER 21 ∗ THE WISDOM OF NATIONS

"WEALTH MAY PROTECT A NATION

Without perseverance, talent is a barren bed.

THE WISDOM OF NATIONS * SEPTEMBER 22

BUT WISDOM PRESERVES A NATION"

Advice is like a stranger; if he's welcomed he stays for the night; if not, he leaves the same day.

SEPTEMBER 23 ✴ THE WISDOM OF NATIONS

"WEALTH MAY PROTECT A NATION

Because he lost his reputation, he lost a kingdom.

THE WISDOM OF NATIONS ✳ SEPTEMBER 24

BUT WISDOM PRESERVES A NATION"

Yesterday is ashes; tomorrow wood. Only today does the fire burn brightly.

SEPTEMBER 25 ✷ THE WISDOM OF NATIONS

"WEALTH MAY PROTECT A NATION

A thief believes everybody steals.

THE WISDOM OF NATIONS * SEPTEMBER 26

BUT WISDOM PRESERVES A NATION"

A wise man never knows all, only fools know everything.

SEPTEMBER 27 * THE WISDOM OF NATIONS

"WEALTH MAY PROTECT A NATION

When angry, Count 10 before you speak; if very angry, 100. If you are patient in a moment of anger, you will escape 100 days of sorrow.

THE WISDOM OF NATIONS ∗ SEPTEMBER 28

BUT WISDOM PRESERVES A NATION"

A close friend can become a close enemy. As the best wine makes the sharpest vinegar, the truest lover may turn into the worst enemy.

SEPTEMBER 29 ✶ THE WISDOM OF NATIONS

"WEALTH MAY PROTECT A NATION

While the blanket is short, learn to bend.

THE WISDOM OF NATIONS * SEPTEMBER 30

BUT WISDOM PRESERVES A NATION"

What ripens quickly, rots quickly.

OCTOBER 1 * THE WISDOM OF NATIONS

"WEALTH MAY PROTECT A NATION

Time spent with family is worth every second.

THE WISDOM OF NATIONS ★ OCTOBER 2

BUT WISDOM PRESERVES A NATION"

Money grows on the tree of persistence.

OCTOBER 3 ✻ THE WISDOM OF NATIONS

"WEALTH MAY PROTECT A NATION

A child without education is like a bird without wings.

THE WISDOM OF NATIONS ⁎ OCTOBER 4

BUT WISDOM PRESERVES A NATION"

He who doesn't go to war roars like a lion.

OCTOBER 5 ✶ THE WISDOM OF NATIONS

"WEALTH MAY PROTECT A NATION

Time and words can't be recalled, even if it was only yesterday.

THE WISDOM OF NATIONS ✳ **OCTOBER 6**

BUT WISDOM PRESERVES A NATION"

The fool speaks. The wise man listens.

OCTOBER 7 * THE WISDOM OF NATIONS

"WEALTH MAY PROTECT A NATION

Do not
look
where
you fell,
but
where
you slipped.

THE WISDOM OF NATIONS ⁕ OCTOBER 8

BUT WISDOM PRESERVES A NATION"

Four things never come back: the spoken word, the spent arrow, the past, the neglected opportunity.

OCTOBER 9 * THE WISDOM OF NATIONS

"WEALTH MAY PROTECT A NATION

The only insurance against fire is to have two houses.

THE WISDOM OF NATIONS ✷ OCTOBER 10

BUT WISDOM PRESERVES A NATION"

If you make a habit of buying things you don't need, you will soon be selling things you do need.

OCTOBER 11 ∗ THE WISDOM OF NATIONS

"WEALTH MAY PROTECT A NATION

A wise man doesn't see his foot on the ground, he watches his next step.

THE WISDOM OF NATIONS ✲ OCTOBER 12

BUT WISDOM PRESERVES A NATION"

Money does not change men, it only unmasks them.

OCTOBER 13 ✳ THE WISDOM OF NATIONS

"WEALTH MAY PROTECT A NATION

Education is an ornament in prosperity and a refuge in adversity.

THE WISDOM OF NATIONS ✶ OCTOBER 14

BUT WISDOM PRESERVES A NATION"

The world is a ladder, in which some go up and others go down.

OCTOBER 15 * THE WISDOM OF NATIONS

"WEALTH MAY PROTECT A NATION

If nakedness promises to cloth you, please be mindful of her name.

THE WISDOM OF NATIONS ✻ OCTOBER 16

BUT WISDOM PRESERVES A NATION"

Dine with a stranger but save your love for your family.

OCTOBER 17 ✷ THE WISDOM OF NATIONS

"WEALTH MAY PROTECT A NATION

Eat when the food is ready; speak when the time is right.

THE WISDOM OF NATIONS * OCTOBER 18

BUT WISDOM PRESERVES A NATION"

If things are getting easier, maybe you are headed downhill.

OCTOBER 19 ✷ THE WISDOM OF NATIONS

"WEALTH MAY PROTECT A NATION

Adversity comes with instruction in his hand.

THE WISDOM OF NATIONS ✷ OCTOBER 20

BUT WISDOM PRESERVES A NATION"

Gold and silver are tested by fire, but we are tested by praise.

OCTOBER 21 ✷ THE WISDOM OF NATIONS

"WEALTH MAY PROTECT A NATION

All food is fit to eat, but not all words are fit to speak.

THE WISDOM OF NATIONS * OCTOBER 22

BUT WISDOM PRESERVES A NATION"

A woman is a flower in a garden; her husband is the fence around it.

OCTOBER 23 ✷ THE WISDOM OF NATIONS

"WEALTH MAY PROTECT A NATION

While two dogs are fighting for a bone, a third runs away with it. When brothers fight to death, a stranger inherits their property.

THE WISDOM OF NATIONS ✷ OCTOBER 24

BUT WISDOM PRESERVES A NATION"

In order to
capture
a city,
first
capture
the heart
of the people.

OCTOBER 25 ✢ THE WISDOM OF NATIONS

"WEALTH MAY PROTECT A NATION

A friend to everybody is a friend to nobody. A friend to all is a friend to none.

THE WISDOM OF NATIONS ✷ OCTOBER 26

BUT WISDOM PRESERVES A NATION"

Do not seek to follow in the footsteps of the men of old; seek what they sought.

OCTOBER 27 ✷ THE WISDOM OF NATIONS

"WEALTH MAY PROTECT A NATION

Speak softly and carry a big stick; you will go far.

THE WISDOM OF NATIONS ✳ OCTOBER 28

BUT WISDOM PRESERVES A NATION"

Whoever trusts his own heart is a fool. Whoever walks in wisdom will survive.

OCTOBER 29 ✵ THE WISDOM OF NATIONS

"WEALTH MAY PROTECT A NATION

Abuse often starts with praise.

THE WISDOM OF NATIONS ☆ OCTOBER 30

BUT WISDOM PRESERVES A NATION"

Work like a slave and eat like a gentleman.

OCTOBER 31 ✶ THE WISDOM OF NATIONS

BUT WISDOM PRESERVES A NATION"

Adversity and loss make a man wise.

NOVEMBER 1 ⁕ THE WISDOM OF NATIONS

"WEALTH MAY PROTECT A NATION

If you buy what you don't need, you steal from yourself.

THE WISDOM OF NATIONS ☼ NOVEMBER 2

BUT WISDOM PRESERVES A NATION"

A land in rebellion has many rulers, but a king of wisdom maintains order.

NOVEMBER 3 ✴ THE WISDOM OF NATIONS

"WEALTH MAY PROTECT A NATION

There is more hope for fools than for people who think they are wise.

THE WISDOM OF NATIONS ✴ NOVEMBER 4

BUT WISDOM PRESERVES A NATION"

Three lessons from a dog:

#1. A dog does not bark at its master

#2. A dog will not leave its master because he is poor

#3. A dog never forgets its owner

NOVEMBER 5 ✶ THE WISDOM OF NATIONS

"WEALTH MAY PROTECT A NATION

If you want a well, only dig in one place.

THE WISDOM OF NATIONS * NOVEMBER 6

BUT WISDOM PRESERVES A NATION"

Good perfume is known by its scent rather than by its advertisement.

NOVEMBER 7 ⁕ THE WISDOM OF NATIONS

"WEALTH MAY PROTECT A NATION

When money is not a servant, it is a master.

THE WISDOM OF NATIONS * NOVEMBER 8

BUT WISDOM PRESERVES A NATION"

A ruler who listens to lies will have a corrupt government.

NOVEMBER 9 ✷ THE WISDOM OF NATIONS

"WEALTH MAY PROTECT A NATION

Better to be criticized by a wise person than to be praised by a fool.

BUT WISDOM PRESERVES A NATION"

Politics is a rotten egg; if broken, it stinks.

NOVEMBER 11 ✻ THE WISDOM OF NATIONS

"WEALTH MAY PROTECT A NATION

The smoothest way is full of stones.

THE WISDOM OF NATIONS ☀ NOVEMBER 12

BUT WISDOM PRESERVES A NATION"

Confidence is half of victory.

NOVEMBER 13 ✲ THE WISDOM OF NATIONS

"WEALTH MAY PROTECT A NATION

Wisdom to kings, happiness to people.

THE WISDOM OF NATIONS ∗ NOVEMBER 14

BUT WISDOM PRESERVES A NATION"

Interest
on debts
grow
without rain.

NOVEMBER 15 ✶ THE WISDOM OF NATIONS

"WEALTH MAY PROTECT A NATION

Better ask 10X than go astray 1X.

THE WISDOM OF NATIONS * NOVEMBER 16

BUT WISDOM PRESERVES A NATION"

He that can't endure the bad, will not live to see the good.

NOVEMBER 17 ✲ THE WISDOM OF NATIONS

"WEALTH MAY PROTECT A NATION

If you don't stand for something, you will fall for something.

THE WISDOM OF NATIONS ☼ NOVEMBER 18

BUT WISDOM PRESERVES A NATION"

When a needle falls into a deep well, many people will look into the well, but few will be ready to go down after it.

NOVEMBER 19 ✶ THE WISDOM OF NATIONS

"WEALTH MAY PROTECT A NATION

Tomorrow belongs to those who prepare for it today.
The future is purchased by the present.

THE WISDOM OF NATIONS ✻ NOVEMBER 20

BUT WISDOM PRESERVES A NATION"

Patience is the mother of a beautiful child.

NOVEMBER 21 ⁕ THE WISDOM OF NATIONS

"WEALTH MAY PROTECT A NATION

It
is not
work that kills,
but worry.

THE WISDOM OF NATIONS ✻ NOVEMBER 22

BUT WISDOM PRESERVES A NATION"

If you're not part of the solution, you're part of the problem.

NOVEMBER 23 ✳ THE WISDOM OF NATIONS

"WEALTH MAY PROTECT A NATION

2
good talkers
are not
worth
1
good listener.

THE WISDOM OF NATIONS * NOVEMBER 24

BUT WISDOM PRESERVES A NATION"

Words from the mouth of the wise are gracious, but fools are consumed by their own words.

NOVEMBER 25 * THE WISDOM OF NATIONS

"WEALTH MAY PROTECT A NATION

A kind word warms a man through three winters.

THE WISDOM OF NATIONS ✷ NOVEMBER 26

BUT WISDOM PRESERVES A NATION"

A
life not lived
for others
is not
worth living.

NOVEMBER 27 ✷ THE WISDOM OF NATIONS

"WEALTH MAY PROTECT A NATION

If you are filled with pride, then you will have no room for wisdom.

THE WISDOM OF NATIONS ※ NOVEMBER 28

BUT WISDOM PRESERVES A NATION"

Many students have become kings or queens, but no teachers have.

NOVEMBER 29 ✷ THE WISDOM OF NATIONS

"WEALTH MAY PROTECT A NATION

A man who pays respect to the great paves his own way for greatness.

THE WISDOM OF NATIONS ✳ NOVEMBER 30

BUT WISDOM PRESERVES A NATION"

People won't remember what you said or what you did to them. They just won't forget how you made them feel.

DECEMBER 1 ✷ THE WISDOM OF NATIONS

"WEALTH MAY PROTECT A NATION

Nobody commits adultery, only utter fools.

THE WISDOM OF NATIONS * DECEMBER 2

BUT WISDOM PRESERVES A NATION"

Wood already touched by fire is not hard to set alight.

DECEMBER 3 ✦ THE WISDOM OF NATIONS

"WEALTH MAY PROTECT A NATION

He who is being carried does not realize how far the town is.

THE WISDOM OF NATIONS * DECEMBER 4

BUT WISDOM PRESERVES A NATION"

Ashes fly back into the face of him who throws them.

DECEMBER 5 ✷ THE WISDOM OF NATIONS

"WEALTH MAY PROTECT A NATION

When there is no enemy within, the enemies outside cannot hurt you.

THE WISDOM OF NATIONS ✲ DECEMBER 6

BUT WISDOM PRESERVES A NATION"

When God cooks, you don't see smoke.

DECEMBER 7 * THE WISDOM OF NATIONS

"WEALTH MAY PROTECT A NATION

1 falsehood spoils 1000 truths.

THE WISDOM OF NATIONS ✷ DECEMBER 8

BUT WISDOM PRESERVES A NATION"

Better a diamond with a flaw than a pebble without one.

DECEMBER 9 ❊ THE WISDOM OF NATIONS

"WEALTH MAY PROTECT A NATION

Small men think they are small; great men never know they are great.

THE WISDOM OF NATIONS ✷ DECEMBER 10

BUT WISDOM PRESERVES A NATION"

Truth, not assumption.

DECEMBER 11 ✴ THE WISDOM OF NATIONS

"WEALTH MAY PROTECT A NATION

Solve 1 problem, and you keep 100 others away.

THE WISDOM OF NATIONS ※ DECEMBER 12

BUT WISDOM PRESERVES A NATION"

No matter how tall the mountain is, it cannot block the sun.

DECEMBER 13 ✶ THE WISDOM OF NATIONS

"WEALTH MAY PROTECT A NATION

Tenacity and adversity are old foes.

THE WISDOM OF NATIONS ⁕ DECEMBER 14

BUT WISDOM PRESERVES A NATION"

Don't extinguish what isn't burning you. A little fire that warms is better than a big fire that burns.

DECEMBER 15 * THE WISDOM OF NATIONS

"WEALTH MAY PROTECT A NATION

Good advice is better than gold. Anger is a bad advisor.

Ambition
and revenge
are always
hungry.

"WEALTH MAY PROTECT A NATION

A good neighbour is better than a brother far off.

THE WISDOM OF NATIONS ✷ DECEMBER 18

BUT WISDOM PRESERVES A NATION"

Where you cannot climb over, you must creep under.

DECEMBER 19 ✱ THE WISDOM OF NATIONS

"WEALTH MAY PROTECT A NATION

A good plan today is better than a perfect plan tomorrow.

THE WISDOM OF NATIONS ✷ DECEMBER 20

BUT WISDOM PRESERVES A NATION"

A happy man marries the girl he loves, but a happier man loves the girl he marries.

DECEMBER 21 ✷ THE WISDOM OF NATIONS

"WEALTH MAY PROTECT A NATION

A
large chair
does not
make
a king.

THE WISDOM OF NATIONS * DECEMBER 22

BUT WISDOM PRESERVES A NATION"

You can resist everything except temptation.

DECEMBER 23 ☼ THE WISDOM OF NATIONS

"WEALTH MAY PROTECT A NATION

Build a man a fire, and he'll be warm for a day. Set a man on fire, and he'll be warm for the rest of his life.

THE WISDOM OF NATIONS ⁕ DECEMBER 24

BUT WISDOM PRESERVES A NATION"

The whole world can be conquered with words, not with drawn swords.

DECEMBER 25 * THE WISDOM OF NATIONS

"WEALTH MAY PROTECT A NATION

There are no shortcuts to any place worth going.

THE WISDOM OF NATIONS ✲ DECEMBER 26

BUT WISDOM PRESERVES A NATION"

Tomorrow is pregnant and no one knows what she will give birth to.

DECEMBER 27 ✲ THE WISDOM OF NATIONS

"WEALTH MAY PROTECT A NATION

It's in old kettles that one makes the best soup.

THE WISDOM OF NATIONS * DECEMBER 28

BUT WISDOM PRESERVES A NATION"

A guest sees more in an hour than the host in a year.

DECEMBER 29 ✶ THE WISDOM OF NATIONS

"WEALTH MAY PROTECT A NATION

Everyone comes with baggage. Find someone who loves you enough to help you unpack.

THE WISDOM OF NATIONS ✴ DECEMBER 30

BUT WISDOM PRESERVES A NATION"

Do good because of tomorrow.

DECEMBER 31 ✻ THE WISDOM OF NATIONS

A year has passed, go back to January 1

www.ingramcontent.com/pod-product-compliance
Lightning Source LLC
Chambersburg PA
CBHW021930290426
44108CB00012B/795